"I have known Ben Hudson for almost thirty years. He deeply believes everything he shares in this little book of big ideas and has successfully practiced it. I laughed out loud at Ben's humor and transparency, while being blessed with his practical wisdom and powerful tools. I know you will too. Buy it, read it, and most of all, DO IT. You won't be disappointed!"

    Bob Lewis, President
    LewisLeadership LLC - Consultants in Strategy, Leadership and Change

"This book is from the heart of one who has been there and has helped numerous others navigate through career transition into creating their own destiny. Ben has done an outstanding job of succinctly addressing a complicated and challenging endeavor that has become the norm in the new world of work."

    Steve Spires, Managing Director and President
    BPI Group, Atlanta, GA

"The traditional résumé job search no longer works! This book provides you with a fresh, time-tested method to prove your value to a potential employer via temp-to-perm. Ben was my mentor when I launched my business, and I know from personal experience that if you learn, master and internalize his methodology you will be happy with the results, whether you are launching your own business or seeking to be employed long term."

    Ron Reardon, Founder
    Patents & More, Inc.
    Co-host of *The Launch Hour* on Atlanta Business RadioX

"Ben Hudson writes from years of practical experience in the areas of career decision making and the practical steps to finding a job. I have known Ben personally the past six years, and I highly recommend him and his book to those who want to meaningfully engage in the marketplace.

"Carefully read these pages if you want a jump start to securing work!"

    Boyd Bailey,
    CEO, *Ministry Ventures;*
    President, *Wisdom Hunters, Roswell, GA*

"This book has practical and easy-to-follow applications for anyone searching for full-time or project-based employment. Following Ben's simple yet proven methods will distinguish you as someone who is better, special and different in today's marketplace."

    A. Brian C. Doud, former executive
    The Coca-Cola Company®

"Getting work today is more challenging than it has ever been, and you have to be able to get your head above the crowd. The trick is doing that and remaining true to yourself. If you properly apply the principles this book teaches, you'll get the attention you deserve, the opportunities you are looking for, and the happiness of knowing you're in control."

    Steve Rae, Founder
    ROAM

How to Find Work...
When There Are No Jobs
What Every Jobseeker Needs To Know
About the Job Market of the Future

By Ben Hudson

Second Edition

How to Find Work...
When There Are No Jobs

What Every Jobseeker Needs to Know

Second Edition

Published by:

Bizda Media
620 Edgewater Trail
Atlanta, GA 30328

bizda3@msn.com

Copyright © 2010 by Ben Hudson. All Rights Reserved.

No part of this book may be reproduced in any way without written permission by the Publisher except for brief quotes written in connection with reviews.

Printed and bound in the United States of America
Cover Design by Frazier Marketing & Design LLC

DEDICATION

This book is dedicated to my family and my God.

To my wife who has presented us with four wonderful children and who has faithfully stood by this trying husband for a long time (exact years classified).

To our children who have presented us with equally wonderful spouses and, at this writing, with TWELVE awesome grandchildren...(count 'em)... Cody, Mackenzie, Jade, Benjamin (great name), Sarah Kate, Abigail, Blythe, Howell, Camille, Clar, Cidney and Alden.

And...

To everyone whose lives and careers have been disrupted by the "worst economy since the great depression."

My prayer is that some of the ideas in this publication might help as many as possible.

Ben Hudson

Contents

1. Introduction 9
2. An Inverted Marketplace 15
3. Knowing What You Have To Sell 19
4. Creating Value 45
5. A Different Approach 55
6. The Solutionship™ Process 59
7. Does This Approach Fit You? 69
8. Getting in Front of the Right People 75
9. Finding the Need 93
10. Filling the Need 101
11. Pricing 107
12. Closing the Deal 109
13. Summary 113
14. Making Habits 115

   The Author 119
   Resources 123
   How Much Is Your Time Worth? 132

1.
Introduction

"If you don't quit, don't cheat and don't run home when trouble arrives, you can only win." — S. Long

Congratulations, you are holding a book written by someone who was once publicly told that he was the dumbest guy the man had ever met…and the man who told him so was probably right!

Well, I will never claim to be the sharpest knife in the drawer, but I have been in an awful lot of drawers, alongside a tremendous number of very sharp knives. If, as the Bible states, iron does sharpen iron, I'd like to think some of it sharpened me. With close to twelve years of hands-on experience in over two hundred small business startups, and with career coaching and job placement success in over one thousand instances, chances are pretty good that I <u>can</u> offer a bit of helpful assistance.

It <u>is</u> a fact that I have personally been there in <u>many</u> career-related situations and the processes we are going to discuss here are completely proven…and even guaranteed effective when done properly.

They were not hatched overnight. They were conceived, tested, and refined over a <u>long</u> period of time.

Now, the chances are that many of you will have heard about, read about, or been taught about many of the pieces, but the environments in which they are shared, the exact paths that they follow and the proven results that they have produced may surprise many of you.

This is not just another sales process, similar to consultant selling, solution selling, or spin selling. It is <u>much</u> more than that!

This process...

- is grounded in a "helping others" mindset that <u>proactively</u> reaches <u>out</u> to others with <u>their needs primarily in mind</u>

- has a strong sensitivity to the rapidly changing dynamics of today's employment marketplace factored throughout its routines

- is timely, targeted, and <u>unquestionably</u> proven

What you have here is a simple publication that clearly outlines a step-by-step process for finding work and for generating income in a marketplace where traditional job postings are becoming practically non-existent.

Unlike many sizeable volumes on job hunting, this little book is not intended to be a college course. *How to Find Work...When There Are No Jobs* is specifically designed to provide only the most useful, proven, pragmatic tools, distilled from over 10 years of hands-on delivery to over 1000 clients. These tools, when utilized properly, are guaranteed to place you in full charge of your career, help you more fully appreciate exactly what benefits you have to offer, know where your best opportunities are, how to get in front of the right people, how to help them surface their most attractive needs, and how to help them fill those needs in a distinctively different manner. They will position you as a unique solutions helper with little or no risk or commitment on the employer's part. They will also teach you how to facilitate the employer's closing decision while allowing them to retain a strong sense of ownership in the entire process.

Simply stated, the overall approach is "temp to perm" with project consulting and contracting being the interim step. The basic concepts are widely accepted but the *Solutionship™ Process* is unique. Solutionship™ is exactly what it says…"a solution developed in partnership" but without all of the objectionable conventional selling methods. These methods are a major hindrance to hundreds of thousands of individuals whose belief is that "there are just not any jobs out there."

The fact is that this assumption is only partially true. There are few traditional job postings "out there." But there are many, many "needs/opportunities in every discipline." They just have to be "surfaced." The Solutionship™ Process is not designed to get anyone a permanent job initially. It is intended to get your foot in the door to generate income and to move you to the front of the line for permanent employment.

You will be taught the entire process here and encouraged to practice it until it becomes intuitive. Only then can you effectively deliver it.

Folks, this Solutionship™ Process works. It has been demonstrated to work both for me and for the many hundreds of individuals I've worked with through the years. This little book can be a turning point in your career, but it must be tried!

As we all know, no program, no process, no method, no procedure will work itself…there just ain't no silver bullets!

Many years back, I stood up in an AA meeting after over two years of sporadic attendance and obnoxiously said, "This program might help some people who really need it, but it just doesn't work for me!"

Immediately, a frail, haggard little guy, who looked like he had been living in his clothes for months, jumped up, got right in my face, and calmly, but loud enough to be heard across the entire room, said, "Mister, you are probably the dumbest (blank) I have ever come across!"

A little shocked, I haughtily responded, "How the heck can you say anything like that?" To which he shouted back, " 'Cause the program don't work for nobody. You've got to work the program!"

He was dead right…on both counts.

This experience was close to twenty-five years ago, but for this dumb (blank) the truth still rings clear.

Any program, like any idea, is inert. It is not worth a plugged nickel until someone genuinely gives it a try…until they work the program!

2.
An Inverted Marketplace

"Inferior minds complicate simple issues. Exceptional minds simplify complicated ones." — Anonymous

We currently find ourselves in an economic situation and a job search environment that may be unprecedented in our lifetimes.

Once upon a time, job security was an accepted fact. You <u>got</u> a good education. You <u>got</u> a good job. You <u>did</u> a good job, and you were set for life.

If you chose to consider a job change, you simply put together a résumé that outlined all of your features, such as your job history, your education, your interests, etc., and circulated that résumé to the companies that had needs that your features fit. An interview was scheduled; the institution decided how well your features fit their needs and then made the job offer decisions.

It was simple, straightforward, and required little need assessment on the part of the potential employee.

In the 1970s, an industry called "outplacement" began to emerge around the employment process. Its primary function was to provide more effective ways for a job seeker to match and fit an employer's job description. Then came head hunters, job fairs, and online job and career sites. The basic process still revolved around the need residing with the employer and the solution being a prospective employee with a <u>feature-laden</u> <u>résumé</u>… a "solution looking for a problem."

Current economic times appear to be, literally, turning the job market upside down. All of the traditional search methods are becoming less and less effective. The conventional résumé-based, interview hiring model is no longer meeting marketplace needs and appears simply to be <u>outdated.</u>

The good news is that even if the jobs are going away, the <u>needs</u> are not going away and, <u>as is true in all change, opportunities abound</u>.

The successful job seeker today will need to do what every successful business has done since businesses began: <u>find the need</u>…<u>and fill it</u>. They will have to assume responsibility for both ends of the process, and will do it in a way that clearly demonstrates their value or return on investment (R.O.I.).

Simply put, this is just a proven <u>entrepreneurial</u> approach to job searching!

The additional good news is that very few of

the thousands of jobseekers, <u>in every job category</u>, understand this, and <u>fewer still</u> know how to make it happen.

You can be one of the individuals who do.

This inverted search market is not likely to reverse itself. The proactive jobseeker who is willing to "seize the day" will not only be successful, they will be able to structure a unique selling proposition (U.S.P.) for themselves that will be <u>extremely</u> attractive in a marketplace overwhelmingly populated by "solutions looking for problems."

3.
Knowing What You Have to Sell

"All truths are easy to understand once they are discovered. The point is to discover them." — Galileo

Everything you, your family, your friends, etc., have ever paid money for was not because of the features of the products or services, but for the *real* and *perceived* benefits they offered.

You didn't purchase your car because it had round rubber things on each corner, your shirt because it had buttons, or your house because it had a roof, etc. These are all simply features. You purchased your car because it made you feel exciting. You purchased your shirt because it matched your suits. You purchased your house to provide comfortable shelter. These are real and perceived benefits.

Most candidate résumés are just a chronologically arranged list of job history, education, awards, and interests. <u>All</u> <u>are</u> <u>features</u> and of <u>little</u> <u>value</u> in today's purchase decisions.

In today's marketplace, you must take the time to clearly understand the <u>benefits</u> <u>that</u> <u>you</u> <u>offer.</u> Our purpose is twofold. First, you need to know the <u>true value</u> that you bring and the fact that, regardless of your background/work history, <u>you have many transferable skill sets</u> that can be brought into new situations. (However, understand that once you have outlined these benefits, they are not just to be dumped in front of a prospect. That would be just another solution, looking for a problem.)

When you have defined your <u>benefits for yourself,</u> they will be extremely helpful in developing the ideas that you and your partner/prospect will surface together.

(See the *Features and Benefits Alignment* chart on page 33.)

I want you to stop, get a copy of your most recent résumé, a legal pad, and begin outlining your transferable business benefits. Go through your résumé and identify situations where your features were utilized. Don't be shy. This is very important and for your usage only. Now, list all of the benefits your features made possible.

When this is done, you might be surprised at your benefits…and the ease with which you can then define the value they can bring.

Benefits Determination

To demonstrate the simplicity of determining your benefits, I have included a couple sample résumés (pp. 23-29) from which I have inventoried some of their benefits, using the *Features and Benefits Alignment* chart.

As you complete yours, ideas will arise that can make it more comprehensive. As already mentioned, this list is for your information and can be extremely helpful in understanding how transferable and valuable your benefits can be in almost every business (or personal) interaction you might incur.

It's a very simple but very beneficial exercise.

For help, refer to *Benefits/Transferable Skills Inventory* section beginning on page 39.

TIM SMITH

123 Street • Chicago, IL 12345 • tim@yahoo.com • (123) 456-7890

APPLICATION DEVELOPER with 5+ Years expertise in multi-platform environments, object oriented application development, and multi-tiered web application design and development.

SUMMARY OF QUALIFICATIONS

- Development and maintenance of custom utilities in multi-platform environments.
- Designed and developed multi-tiered Web application using Java
- Capable of full life cycle systems analysis and design.
- 4 years expertise in utilizing OOAD skills
- 4 years of SQL and PL/SQL using Oracle 8i and 9i
- 2 years of Java, 2 years C++, and 1 year C# experience
- 2 years using MQ series to pass and retrieve information

TECHNICAL SKILLS

PLATFORMS AND TOOLS
- **SOFTWARE:** Jbuilder, Visual Age, Visual Studio .NET, MS Office, Frontpage
- **DATABASE:** Oracle, Access, PL/SQL, SQL Server 2000
- **APPLICATION DEVELOPMENT:** .Net, J2EE, ASP, NET, JSP, XML C, Visual C++, C# Java, Html, Ajax, Javascript, VB6, VB.net, CORBA, Roguewave and Rationalrose
- **OTHER:** MS Project Management

PROFESSIONAL EXPERIENCE

SOFTWARE ENGINEER   Month 200X - Present
COMPANY   Chicago, IL

- Enhanced functionality of investigative software for the Department.
- Designed system for one-stop online access for employee background verifications.
- System specially designed with full online capabilities for recruitment purposes.

SOFTWARE ENGINEER   Month 200X – Month 200X
COMPANY   Chicago, IL

TIM SMITH • tim@yahoo.com • (123) 456-7890 • Page 2

- Integrated ASP.Net, C#, HTML and Javascript resulting in an improved Pricing Application.
- Enhanced pricing system allowed the sales team to access online quotes and contracts within a short time frame.
- Allowed Sales Representatives to illustrate the most cost effective means of pricing data lines.

SOFTWARE ENGINEER Month 200X – Month 200X
COMPANY Chicago, IL

- Maintained and developed custom utilities in a multi-platform environment proprietary software.
- Formalized the programming, unit testing and system documentations for existing products.
- Used .Net Framework including ASP, VB.Net, with Oracle 9i database

SOFTWARE ENGINEER Month 200X – Month 200X
CORPORATION Chicago, IL

- Developed and maintained a cataloging system using PL/SQL in an Oracle relational database.
- Administered the analysis, design, programming, unit testing and system documentation functions.
- Created a multi-tiered Web Application using J2EE framework.
- Produced and implemented a Java based Passive Surveillance System (PSS) prototype using Java.

APPLICATIONS PROGRAMMER Month 199X – Month 200X
COMPANY Chicago, IL

- Created multi-tiered applications using OOAD programming standards, C++ mid-tier, and Oracle.
- Prepared formal presentations for management and peer levels.
- Utilized NT and Unix platforms.

EDUCATION AND TRAINING

BACHELOR OF SCIENCE-COMPUTER INFORMATION SYSTEMS 199X
UNIVERSITY Chicago, IL

Business Administration

Melissa M. Beck
450 Fenway Apt. 7 | Boston, MA 02115
beck.m@gmail.com | (617) 629 - 4244

Education

Northeastern University Boston, MA
Bachelor of Science in Business Administration May 2008
Dual Concentration: Marketing and Entrepreneurship
GPA 3.6, Dean's List, Marketing Club

Professional Experience

Northeastern University Department of Career Services Boston, MA
Marketing Assistant Jan. 2008 - Present

- Design marketing materials such as flyers, event posters, emails and online newsletters using MS Publisher
- Produce electronic multimedia displays utilizing MS PowerPoint to market events across campus
- Assist in event coordination including working with printing vendors

Samsonite Mansfield, MA
Retail Marketing Assistant Jan. - June 2007

- Assisted with development of Customer Relations Management Program initiative
- Contributed on the production of the holiday catalog, including photo-shoots, content and layout
- Received and responded to donation requests
- Conducted research for possible cross promotions and partner marketing
- Researched competitor best-practices prior to the introduction of new product lines
- Designed a store level Product Knowledge Guide and several product description sheets
- Acted as liaison between store managers and corporate office for individual marketing requests
- Created and administered surveys to over 180 stores to solve store related issues
- Monitored development of MS Access inventory management and forecasting program

Stacy's Pita Chip Company Randolph, MA
Gourmet Account Manager Jan. - Aug. 2006

- Managed 50+ gourmet retail accounts including: corporate, restaurant, and specialty store
- Represented and promoted the company and its product lines at the Fancy Food Trade Show
- Assisted customer service department with fulfilling donation requests
- Aided the sales department by constructing sample boxes and press packets
- Utilized Excel and QuickBooks to create reports to track budget and performance goals for the VP of Sales
- Documented and resolved buyer and consumer issues and concerns
- Entered sales orders, created invoices, and received payments in QuickBooks

Business Administration

Accounts Payable

- Assisted Accounts Receivable Manager using Electronic Data Interchange to process accounts receivable
- Tracked incoming inventory and assisted trouble-shooting when discrepancies arose by working with vendors and the head of manufacturing

New City Beauty Salon and Supplies New City, NY
Retail Associate 1998 – 2002; June – Aug. 2003

- Collaborated with L'Oreal representative to revamp entire L'Oreal stock and display
- Created attractive product displays to increase product awareness
- Handled the needs of a 10 person salon staff while also assisting retail customers
- Trained new employees, managed merchandise orders and handled opening/closing of store

Other Experiences

- Teachers Apprentice Program, teaching sixth grade students American Sign Language Spring 2002
- Produced a Red Cross fundraiser for the World Trade Center Relief Fall 2001

Skills

- MS Access, Excel, Word, PowerPoint, Publisher, Outlook, Lotus Notes, QuickBooks, Adobe Photoshop
- American Sign Language

Resume courtesy of Northeastern University Career Center

JobWeb.com—Career development and job-search advice for new college graduates.
Copyright © National Association of Colleges and Employers
62 Highland Ave • Bethlehem, PA 18017-9085
Phone: 610/868-1421 or 800/544-5272 • Fax: 610/868-0208
Privacy Policy • Contact Us

Tim Smith

Benefits

- **Analytical**
- **Creative**
- **Financial Management**
- **Perceptive**
- **Planner, Organizer**
- **Strategic Thinker**

Melissa Beck

Benefits

- **Creative**
- **Writer**
- **Influencer**
- **Diplomatic**
- **Listening Ability**
- **Perceptive**
- **Planner, Organizer**

Features and Benefits Alignment

Business Benefits	Features
Analytical	• Identifies skills and patterns • Reviews reports • Researches/compares suppliers • Assesses opportunities and risks
Coaching	• Helps others develop • Serves as a team leader • Identifies training and development needs for self, partners, and employees • Motivates others

Business Benefits	Features
Creative	- Generates innovative ideas and solutions - Manages cash flow - Identifies barter opportunities - Decorates the office - Entertains on a budget - Performs sales, promotion and marketing
Decisiveness	- Refuses to be plagued by analysis paralysis - Takes risks - Makes judgment calls - Performs as an effective leader
Diplomatic	- Resolves conflicts tactfully - Mediates disputes between vendors, employees or other stakeholders - Negotiates deals with clients and sales management

Business Benefits	Features
Influencing	- Persuades and motivates to sell company's products or services - Communicates mission/vision - Inspires extra effort from team
Listening Ability	- Listens actively - Builds trust (serves in HR functions, account executive or customer service)
Managing Finances	- Understands relationships between balance sheet, income statement, cash flow statement and supporting worksheets - Develops projections and forecasts of financial statements - Performs sensitivity analysis on financial statements

Business Benefits	Features
Networking Skills	• Gives to give, not just to get (serves as Chief networking officer, sales or training team member)
Public Speaking	• Speaks comfortably and assuredly to groups (serves as Company spokesperson or Public Relations representative) • Leads seminars for clients, sales training, sales promotions
Perceptive	• Sensitive to other's needs, thoughts, emotions • Anticipates problems • Proactively looks for solutions • Identifies customer sales opportunities

Business Benefits	Features
Planning and Organizing	• Performs multiple tasks efficiently, effectively and on time (serves in Project management roles, and scheduler/coordinator of special company events
Relationship-Oriented	• Develops, sustains, maintains strategic alliances (serves in sales, sales management and business development)
Strategic	• Sees the big picture (serves in Operations, marketing, long-range planning, management)
Team-Building	• Collaborates to achieve goals • Possesses the ability to bring people to work together for a common goal • Fosters camaraderie and cohesiveness through strong coaching and communication skills

Business Benefits	Features
Writing	- Communicates clearly with words - Creates written policies and procedures, articles for trade, PR, sales promotion and intercompany news

Benefits/Transferable Skills Inventory

Use this list to assist you in indentifying the skills you have learned or developed through experience. Select the six skills that best describe you. Be sure each skill you select is supported by experience, education or achievements. The list below is necessarily general. It is important that you include any additional skills needed to create an accurate picture of yourself.

Communicating

Corresponding
Drawing
Editing
Facilitating
Interviewing
Listening
Managing conflict
Mediating
Negotiating
Presenting ideas
Public speaking
Relating to customers
Writing
Others:

_____

_____

Coordinating

Cataloging
Correcting
Following up
Recording
Reporting
Scheduling
Others:

_____

_____

Developing People

Assessing performance
Coaching
Counseling
Developing
Helping others
Motivating
Teaching

Team building
Training
Others:
_____
_____

Financial Management

Auditing
Budgeting
Controlling
Cost accounting
Financial analysis
Financial planning
Fund raising
Managing finance
Others:
_____
_____

Managing Data

Analyzing data
assessing quality
Computing
Gathering data
Managing information
Measuring
Research
Setting standards
Taking inventory
Others:
_____
_____

Managing/Directing

Approving
Delegating
Developing procedures
Developing systems
Directing
Formulating
Implementing
Instructing
Interpreting policy
Making decisions
Managing details
Managing people
Managing projects
Managing tasks
Revitalizing
Serving as change agent
Others:
_____
_____

Organizing

Administering
Assigning
Categorizing
Developing work plans
Projecting
Restructuring
Setting priorities
Others:
_____
_____

Planning

Analyzing
Conceptualizing
Designing
Developing policy
Developing strategy
Reviewing
Surveying
Others:

_____

_____

Selling/Marketing

Advertising
Analyzing markets
Managing sales
Marketing
Pricing
Promoting
Relating to clients
Selling
Writing proposals
Others:

_____

_____

Serving

Client relations
Handling complaints
Responding promptly
Serving customers
Others:

_____

_____

Technical Skills

Computer literate
Designing
Designing systems
Developing products
Engineering
Inventing
Scientific research
Manufacturing
Programming
Tooling
Others:

_____

_____

Select the *six* skills that best describe you. Enter them on the lines below.

_____

_____

_____

_____

_____

_____

Of these six, select the *three* that represent your strongest skills and those you most enjoy using. Place a check next to these three.

Assessing your Personal Characteristics

Each of us possesses certain personal characteristics—or traits—that make us unique and enhance our ability to perform different tasks successfully. Review the list below and select the *six* traits that describe you best. Be sure that there is clear evidence of your accomplishments for the traits you check.

accurate	enthusiastic	physically fit
adventurous	expressive	practical
artistic	good attitude	productive
assertive	hard worker	rational
challenging	high standards	responsible
civic-minded	imaginative	responsive
committed	independent	self-assured
communicate well	inquisitive	self-controlled
compassionate	intelligent	self-starter
confident	intuitive	sense of humor
creative	kind	sensitive
curious	leader	sociable
dedicated	levelheaded	stable
dependable	loyal	tolerant
efficient	original	trustworthy
emotional	people-oriented	others:
energetic	perfectionist	_____
entertaining	personable	
	persuasive	_____

Select the *six* traits that describe you best. Enter them on the lines below.

_____

_____

_____

_____

_____

Of these six, select the *three* that represent your most prominent traits and place a check next to them.

You can learn more about yourself by reviewing the above list again. This time look for a trait that may be considered something an interviewer could see as a weakness.

4.
Creating Value
by Consulting/Contracting

"We make our living by what we get, but we make our life by what we give." — Anonymous

Almost all of us who consult for a living spend a great deal of time thinking about how we can create value for our clients. That's how we earn our keep. Yet, every idea we come up with seems to always consist of some mixture of the same three broad possibilities. We create value by

- being the **expert**
- being a skilled **pair of hands**
- being a **facilitator**

We usually bring some special knowledge, or know-how to the situation, often help with some of the application work requested by the client, and spend time drawing out information and insights from client personnel while helping them follow a process of discovery that leads to change.

Although most assignments involve a mixture of these roles, it is important to be aware of <u>where</u> the emphasis lies, for that is how we determine who has accepted ownership of the problem. Let's look more closely at each of these possibilities.

Expert

This traditionally has been the role most people consider when they think about consulting. Why else would you pay someone unless they were able to tell you something you didn't already know? In the expert role, the consultant takes over responsibility for the problem.

Experts obviously are capable of creating value for a client. Too often, however, it ends up with the consultant producing an answer to the problem as <u>he</u> <u>or</u> <u>she</u> <u>has</u> <u>defined</u> <u>it</u> rather than as the client understands it.

If I defined the problem there is no doubt I could have produced a technically sound solution. And there is little doubt either that it never would be implemented. Consequently, it will be of little, if any, value to the client.

Pair of Hands

When a consultant assumes the pair-of-hands role, just the opposite happens from the expert role. The client remains firmly in control, keeping full responsibility for the problem. Clients often need either skilled people to carry out a task that already has been clearly defined, or someone knowledgeable in a particular subject to conduct specific activities related to that knowledge. Many would argue that the pair-of-hands role is not really consulting, but closer to contract labor. The fact remains that many play this role, and clients value their contributions.

Facilitator

In the facilitator role, the consultant sees his or her role as one of facilitating a change process in which the client and consultant share responsibility. By sharing responsibility, you reduce the risks inherent in the other roles.

In the facilitator role, both consultant and client share a sense of responsibility and both are more likely to contribute their best thinking. The mutual objective is to capitalize on the consultant's knowledge and expertise to fit the client's needs and goals in ways that can work and, most importantly, that lead to implemented solutions that get results. Makes sense, but while people can abstractly comprehend consulting as something other than delivering expertise, most have great difficulty actually doing it.

Acceptance of this role still hasn't improved much. The fact that client-consultant collaboration adds great value to a consulting project does not mean clients will necessarily embrace the approach. And, of course, consultants feel most comfortable going off to do their thing on projects. This is a no-no! It is up to you to make certain the client has a <u>strong sense of ownership</u>!

Consultants must be more than experts in their field. They must serve as effective change agents and <u>share</u> <u>accountability</u> with their clients for the ultimate outcome of their consulting projects while allowing the client to <u>always</u> be the hero.

Please allow me to clarify by discussing a bit about the three value-adding roles of a consultant or contractor.

- **The Expert** – As stated, this is the role that most often comes to mind when consulting or contracting is considered. It is also often a strong hindrance to an individual who is contemplating one or both of those options. In my experience, this stems from the fear that their level of personal knowledge does not reach that of their perception of an "expert" and it simply stops their consideration of this path.

    In reality, most people are not impressed by "what you know". Their primary interest is in "what you do with what you know."

    While everyone should possess some level of special knowledge in some specific areas, true value most often results from some combination of all three roles with the most meaningful contributions weighted toward the latter two.

Also, remember, almost no one likes a "know-it-all expert."

- **Extra Pair of Hands** – While this role might appear to be the least significant value-producer, it can be the most meaningful. Today's corporate environment of layoffs, mergers, acquisitions, etc., has generally thinned the ranks of competent teams and has raised the potential visibility for this service/assistance element substantially. Additionally, its hands-on executorial nature places the "doer" in an area of responsibility that will give them the credibility to recommend improvements, new opportunities, etc., and to enhance the decision makers merit/credibility.

- **Facilitator** – This role can be the most meaningful and valuable of the three and is a function that almost all of us are capable of performing. To be most effective, it will require that we assume a proactive position from the beginning, soliciting input from each of the key players, developing a suggested action plan outline, developing ownership from the teams, establishing time frames and responsibility areas and "coming alongside" each team member. You must be careful not to position yourself as the "boss," but as a "servant" with internal communication structured to allow the credit to fall on the decision maker and your fellow players.

The point of this discussion is simply to re-emphasize that the value you can bring as a project consultant or a contractor is usually much less dependent on high level specialized expertise than it is on helping to implement the program. As has been said many times, ideas are inert and are completely worthless until implemented. In a marketplace where fear of failure leads to reactive immobility, a positive, proactive "doer" mindset stands out in practically every organization as a true value producer!

* * *

The Value of Visioning

We have found that using a form of **visioning** also is an excellent way to help clients begin the change process on their own terms. By getting clients to describe what it would be <u>like</u> to actually achieve the results they would most like to see, you can uncover hidden priorities and subtle details of their desires and concerns. We often ask client executives to write what <u>they</u> <u>would</u> <u>like</u> <u>to</u> <u>read</u> if their publication of choice were to publish an article about the project once it was completed. This, along with an assessment of current realities, provides a solid basis for how the present differs from the future they hope to create with the project. Having these two descriptions – the vision and the current realities – makes it easier to start delineating gaps and to identify what needs to be done to close the gaps.

* * *

Summary

As a consultant/contractor, you create value for your clients by helping them get the results <u>they</u> <u>want.</u> And you greatly improve your chances of doing this when you are able to:

- Use a collaborative facilitator role to deliver your expertise.

- Share responsibility for the problem with your client.

- Use a visioning process to develop a deeper understanding of your client's desires and concerns.

- Remember that results and value are, in the final analysis, defined by your client.

5.
A Different Approach

"We will not solve problems by using the same thinking that created them." — Albert Einstein

Success finding work in today's market will likely require a role reversal on your part. Your first thoughts should no longer be <u>your</u> job objective, <u>your</u> income requirements, <u>your</u> workplace parameters, etc. Your primary focus should be on <u>helping the prospect, not selling them.</u>

Together, you must <u>help</u> surface opportunities in a way that a potential employer can take ownership <u>of the process</u>…and that places you in the <u>potential</u> position of a <u>solutions provider</u>—<u>partner.</u>

It will also be your responsibility to demonstrate your real value and to recommend an engagement process that meets the employer's needs while positioning you at the head of the line if/when a permanent position is a possibility.

I've seen this done many times and am convinced that there is no special gene needed to make it successful. <u>Anyone</u> can benefit who gives it a try.

This approach is usually referred to as "temp-to-perm" with contracting/consulting being the transitional step. Credibility, on both sides, can be developed and it <u>can create high personal visibility</u> if a permanent job is a possibility. (Many permanent jobs now come from this process.)

Individual employer benefits are many. (Contracting/consulting employees are approaching 70% of total employment in Europe and 25–30% in the U.S.)

The advantages for the employee are also very significant. Let's take a moment to look at both and more clearly understand why this different approach makes complete sense.

Why contracting/project consulting rather than just looking for a job?

The reasons for this approach are mentioned throughout this publication, but for emphasis and clarity, I'd like to summarize some of the key ones again. If this approach is to be successful, it is extremely important to keep the reasons/advantages top of mind.

First, from the employer's standpoint:

- *It is more effective.* It allows the employer to concentrate the assistance specifically on the need/opportunity, minimizing distractions and allowing for more effective milestones.

- *It is more efficient.* The investment can be focused specifically on the opportunity and potential expenses, while insurance costs, personal benefits, etc., are minimized.

- *It is politically acceptable.* In most organizations, permanent head count is a "dirty word."

- *It allows for a trial period of employment* – without legal restrictions.

Second, from the employee's standpoint:

- *It is easier to get in front of the decision maker* – with a minimum of defensiveness on their part.

- *It is easier to establish a "service positioning"* – rather than a "selling" positioning.

- *It is easier to actively engage the decision maker* – the Solutionship™ Process can increase the overall effectiveness by eliminating most of the conventional defensive responses.

- *It allows for a "trial period"* – where the employee can assist in "writing his/her own job description" and positioning him/her as an objective third party with no political agenda.

- *There can be significant tax advantages.*

- *Hourly rates can be attractive.*

- *It can offer meaningful flexibility related to additional potential projects.*

We are going to discuss a very effective way to leverage these advantages. Again, it is an easily understood and readily implementable process that is <u>guaranteed</u> to produce results <u>when</u> <u>properly delivered</u>!

6.
The Solutionship™ Process
A proven path to finding work

"Destiny is not a matter of chance; it is a matter of choice. It is not to be waited for; it is a thing to be achieved." — W. S. Bryan

When I left the corporate world, it was <u>certain</u> that I was to be God's gift to consulting. Unfortunately, my ego made the path almost impossible. I am now certain that I probably made almost every mistake in the book.

Before leaving The Coca-Cola Company,® I was asked to take responsibility for a rather significant project. This stroke of luck, unfortunately, confirmed my illusions regarding the riches that awaited me. I rented a large office, bought a room full of furniture, hired a secretary and hung a huge shingle: Business Development Associates, Ben Hudson, President. I then started walking the halls of The Company (Coke®) telling all my associates how smart I was and how dumb they were to stay in the corporate world.

The project lasted for a year, and actually went pretty well; but as soon as it ended, <u>I did not have a clue</u> where to go from there. I had $3,500 a month in overhead and went over thirteen months without earning a single additional dime…<u>some gift to consulting</u>!

I tried everything I thought a brilliant consultant would do. I spent close to $10,000 on professional, four-color collateral materials.

I identified over a hundred target companies that I knew would be clamoring for my expertise.

I identified the key decision makers in marketing, sales, promotions and operations.

I sent each of them my exceptional collateral package and personal cover letters via overnight mail. I told each of them I would be contacting them right away. I grouped them into manageable groups and began the process of going to market.

Surprisingly, I got through to a good percentage of them and even received some excellent comments—"Well done," "very professional package," etc.—as well as a number of others that all said basically the same thing—"Thanks for the material. We don't have anything right now but will keep it on file and be in touch if anything comes up."

Yeah, right…after contacting over half of my targets, I suddenly realized <u>I hadn't been asked to come see a single person!</u> Then the brilliant thought struck me, should I have <u>asked them</u> for an appointment?

I reversed course, attempting to re-contact and <u>get in to see them</u>…and guess what, most of them did not even have the courtesy to return my calls. Imagine that!

<u>Then</u> it occurred to me that presenting Ben Hudson as the "solution looking for a problem" might not be exactly the right approach. So, I began trying to think of some of the things that I might have learned over the year and a half. Here are a few of those brilliant insights:

- Rather than continue to re-invent the consulting wheel, talking to someone who had a successfully established practice might be helpful.

- Maybe I don't need an 800 square foot office, a secretary, expensive furniture, etc. I had had <u>one</u> potential client (a personal friend) visit me.

And…

- Since my single biggest problem was <u>credibility,</u> maybe I should try to find what it would take to get in front of decision makers, with <u>their needs</u> in mind and to establish some sort of relationship. Maybe I should even try to figure out <u>how</u> <u>I</u> <u>might</u> <u>help</u> <u>them,</u> rather than selling them my "awesome expertise."

Over the next year, I did manage to pick up a few projects and begin to learn what it took to <u>really help</u>

folks, and, <u>most importantly</u>, how to develop trusting, meaningful relationships.

Since that time, with the help of a lot of folks much smarter than I, the process began working and has evolved into what we call "The Solutionship™ Process."

This approach is just what is says…it is <u>a **solution** developed in partner**ship**.</u>

It has now been shared with over a thousand individuals with exceptional results.

The Solutionship™ Process just <u>works</u>…because it is based on relational, common sense, proven elements that have demonstrated their effectiveness many, many times.

The first essential requirement is for the entire interaction to simply come off as a <u>personal conversation</u> facilitated by an interested friend, with <u>as few sales overtones as possible. This is extremely important</u> if the results are to be maximized. <u>The minute the interaction begins to sound like a sales pitch, its effectiveness nosedives.</u>

We have seen that <u>almost anyone</u> can become proficient in this conversation development; and that <u>everyone</u>, no matter the experience level, can benefit tremendously. Practice is essential, and, the best people to practice on <u>are always</u> simply the people you know the best: family, friends, or business associates can all help, as long as they have a basic understanding of business.

Once the proper comfort level is reached, it should then be committed to a habit. There is a section on habit building at the end of the book.

The second critical piece is the interview process itself. Most of you will recognize the well-proven SWOT analysis. (We will also walk through a demonstration of how I deliver it.)

Whenever possible, a social beginning is always a good way to begin. Start with a personal opening and transition to a leadership/facilitator role as soon as possible. This is also a good time to establish the fact that <u>you are there to help and not to sell</u>. I usually tell them that if any ideas are surfaced that they like, but outside help is currently precluded, <u>they are welcome to them</u>!

This will reduce defensiveness and can position you as a truly <u>different type of resource.</u>

In all the years I have done it, it has <u>never</u> backfired. I have <u>never</u> had anyone take advantage of the situation.

The SWOT Analysis

S – Strengths

The first question is only to get the client talking positively about themselves and their business, something like, "Tell me what is going really well within the business right now" and other "probing around" issues where you might have expertise. The object is simply to make them comfortable and to <u>encourage</u> <u>bragging</u> to set up the transition to the "W" section.

W – Weaknesses/Needs

When the timing is right, we transition to the weakness/need (W) area by saying something like: "Congratulations! That sounds <u>great</u>. But while we're here, do you mind talking about a few things that aren't going as well as you would like…things that you might like to see some improvement in?"

This is the "red meat" section: I will write down <u>direct</u> <u>quotes</u> but <u>focus</u> only <u>on</u> <u>2-3</u> <u>issues.</u>

Before going further, let's expand on the "W" section…

The "Red Meat" Opportunities

The objective in this "W" portion of the SWOT analysis is to identify no more than three "potential areas for improvement." As mentioned, the first couple will generally be the ones that are top of mind to the "interviewee" and you should facilitate the conversation to eliminate an extensive list where prioritization becomes an issue. You should simply agree on a broad description of two or three needs/opportunities and obtain a <u>verbatim statement</u> from your client outlining them <u>in their words</u>. Don't attempt to get too deeply into the details in this session; they will come in the discovery phase of the deliverables in your letter of understanding "note."

These "red meat" opportunities might or might not fall within your strongest expertise areas. If they do not, you can always bring in sub-contracting help while continuing to be the "resource." Your number one objective is to identify an opportunity area where you can truly be of service. If you don't find a project, a strong networking contact is <u>always</u> worth the time spent.

The needs/opportunities can vary widely – sales, marketing, IT, training, financial, etc. If you honestly feel that it is completely outside your area of expertise and you have absolutely no way of bringing in a sub-contractor to assist, follow up with a second meeting and/or email and simply tell them the truth.

Thank them for their time and feedback in your interview and keep the door open for another networking contact.

In the Solutionship™ Process there is no such thing as a "rejection."

O – Opportunities

Once the needs are defined, we transition to the opportunities (O) area by saying something like, "Thanks for the input, but while I'm here, tell me about some opportunities that you can see in the next year or so."

Write down the quotations and discuss as appropriate.

T – Threats

When we have the information needed to consider a solution, we move to the threats (T) with a question like: "What is keeping you from taking advantage of these opportunities?" The usual answer is people, time, money, etc.

The Proposal Setup

<u>We should try not to talk solutions</u>. Instead, say something like, "This has been really great. I'd like to make a suggestion. Let me think about it for a day or so and come back to you with some ideas."

Set a date/time, shake their hand…and <u>leave!</u>

The Success Mindset

As we have said, there are no magic bullets, but the Solutionship™ Process does work if you work it....

Just remember:

It takes frequency.

It takes familiarity.

It takes regularity.

It takes time.

It takes effort.

It takes risk.

It takes asking the right questions.

It takes listening for and hearing others' real needs.

It takes trust.

It takes integrity.

It takes…but it gives…much, much more.

It is about your true business character…what you are willing to do "<u>when you are certain nobody else is looking</u>."

It is about sharing, but with the humility to truly serve and to let others be the HERO. Robert Woodruff, one of the great presidents of The Coca-Cola Company® said, "There is no limit to what a man can do or how far he can go if he doesn't mind who gets the credit."

Finally, it is about friendship and <u>relationship, not selling!</u>

That old bugaboo <u>rejection</u> is a non-issue, even if a deal is not the end result. An exceptional networking contact can <u>always be just as important</u>!

7.
Does This Approach Fit You?

At some point, we usually ask ourselves this question: "Does this approach fit me?"

Over the years, I have often heard comments like, "I have never been a consultant," or "I'm not sure consulting or contracting is the right approach for someone with my background or at my level."

I am convinced that it can meaningfully help almost <u>anyone,</u> at <u>any</u> level, in <u>any</u> discipline. Let me share three success stories, involving three distinctly different disciplines and three widely varied levels of responsibility.

A C-level individual whose income approached a million dollars annually.

This man was a distinguished gentleman, obviously very intelligent, who walked into my office and immediately apologized by saying, "Ben, I am just wasting your time." When asked to explain, he said that he was financially secure, fifty-seven years old, but just not ready to quit. He said that he didn't know anything he could do except consult and at his age and background, he was <u>not</u> going to do anything that might make a fool out of him. Then he said, "I've never done any consulting and don't know anything about it, so I guess that even eliminates this option." He said that the only reason he stopped by was to pacify his coach.

I asked him if he would be willing to play a game with me relating to consulting. As we seemed to have hit it off, he said he'd at least listen.

I asked him if he had two to three friends to whom he'd be willing to just tell the truth. His response was, "Maybe. What do you mean?"

I asked if he'd let me take him through a process called The Solutionship™ and then get him to tell two to three friends exactly what he just told me, asking for their feedback, <u>nothing else.</u> He laughingly agreed and we set a time three weeks out to get back together.

He called me at the end of his conversations and said that the feedback had been a lot of fun and that, incredibly, "there may even be a little project work here." I suggested that he follow up and keep me posted. He did, we met several more times, and over the next twelve months, he got three projects, with a total income of close to $300,000! (Now I'm not suggesting that this will be the result every time, but in his case, it wasn't bad.)

A middle manager, early 40s, who had spent his career in field sales and marketing, moved all over the country, and had just moved to Atlanta.

When this man put together his networking contact list, he didn't think he had any corporate decision maker links and that the Solutionship™ Process would not be of any help to him.

I asked him if he knew anyone in any smaller companies that might, at least, be willing to give him some feedback.

We came up with a friend involved in a startup in Charleston, S.C., but one he knew wouldn't be able to afford him. I asked him to just ask his friend for feedback and to make a trip to Charleston. After some practice on the Solutionship™ Process, he went. He called me, the next day, and told me that the friend did need a little help, but that it would take only a couple of weeks. He also told me that he was right; long term, they wouldn't have enough money to hire him. That project lasted three months and was extended to six months. Later, I got a call saying that he had been offered an <u>equity position,</u> and, "what a <u>great place</u> Charleston <u>is</u>."

Pretty exciting stuff.

IT project manager who knew everything, had been a consultant and knew the Solutionship™ Process would not work in the information technology arena.

This man had been in a yearlong outplacement program. He "knew" that because I didn't know anything about his business, spending any time together would be a waste of <u>his</u> time.

After I had reached out to him several times, I got a call telling me that he had a client he needed badly, but he could not get his foot in the door. He again said that he didn't think I could help, but now he'd try anything.

We went through the Solutionship™ Process again and practiced it several times…emphasizing the fact that we had <u>nothing to sell</u> and we were only asking for a few minutes to discuss a couple of ideas that might add directly to the bottom line.

He, somewhat grudgingly, followed our outline.

I then got an email the morning of his appointment with one line: "It went exactly like you scripted it!"… and he got the project!

As we have said, Solutionship™ Process works…at every level…because it is just common sense…needs never go away…we've just got to find them before we can fill them.

8.
Getting in Front of the Right People

"Small opportunities are often the beginning of great enterprises." — Demosthenes

The Coca-Cola Company,® like many Fortune 500 companies, has a space for vendors to wait for their appointments. It's equipped with phones, writing surfaces, internet access, etc.

Almost anytime you stop by, there will usually be one or more vendors reporting back to their boss (or their boss's boss) about a great meeting they just had with a large number of Coke® executives in one of their many conference rooms. In a good number of cases, it will go something like, "We had a terrific meeting <u>with</u> <u>eleven</u> <u>people</u> and they <u>all</u> <u>loved</u> our ideas…and want us to get back to them in the next two to three weeks! If this thing goes the way it sounds like it might, we will make a fortune!"

Unfortunately, most of us know that few times is there a <u>true</u> <u>decision</u> <u>maker</u> in such a session. If anything ever develops, it will take much, much longer to happen and be much, much smaller than ever visualized.

Understanding this does pose the question: <u>How do we</u> get in front of the real decision maker? Obviously, smaller companies, with fewer levels of executives, are somewhat easier, but whether it is Coca-Cola,® General Mills, IBM or a "little" 250 million dollar organization, this fact holds true: obtaining a decision maker's time <u>only</u> <u>comes</u> <u>from</u> <u>one</u> <u>source</u>… <u>networking</u> <u>contacts!</u>

People <u>we</u> <u>know</u> who <u>are</u> decision makers, or people <u>we</u> <u>know</u> who <u>know</u> the decision makers are the <u>only</u> way!

If the Solutionship™ Process is the path you choose, your single biggest hurdle is not expertise, credentials, or a presentation package (website, printed collateral, etc.). It is <u>your</u> <u>credibility;</u> and **this hurdle is <u>only</u> overcome by <u>demonstrating</u> <u>your</u> <u>value</u> to someone who can approve an invoice**.

Effective networking <u>is</u> the answer, and the process is extremely straightforward. I have included information to help you develop your personal network. It <u>is</u> simple, not necessarily easy, but absolutely proven effective!

In most cases, it is a good idea to initially disregard the <u>huge</u> <u>potential</u> opportunities where the line is long. <u>Simply</u> <u>start</u> <u>with</u> <u>people</u> <u>who</u> <u>you</u> <u>know</u> <u>the</u> <u>best</u>… places where you can get some time to practice it to a <u>solid</u> <u>comfort</u> <u>level.</u> The first few folks you see won't even need to be decision makers, just friends, family, etc. – folks who can give you some helpful feedback and with whom you can have a comfortable, conversational meeting.

It might be something like, "I'm thinking about looking for some project consulting work and I've got a process I'd like to get your feedback on!"

Tell them the truth! Keep it simple! Treat them like a real prospect and get started.

Once you get comfortable, you are ready for real prospects. But, always <u>begin</u> <u>small</u>. It will be <u>faster, more productive</u> and possibly even surprising!

Getting In Front of the Right People
REMINDERS

➢ To successfully utilize the Solutionship™ Process and land a consulting or contracting project, the "right person" will vary as you move through the processes.

➢ Initially, you must simply develop a level of familiarity and confidence in your delivery that can naturally evolve into an <u>amicable personal conversation</u>, one with <u>any sense of selling or salesmanship removed</u>!

➢ In this first situation you should start with three or four individuals who understand the rudiments of business but with whom you feel absolutely comfortable. You get there by just telling them the facts (you are thinking about looking for consulting or contract work and have a process you'd like to practice on them). Treat them like an actual prospect, ask them for feedback… but remember that your primary objective in this case is practice (but <u>do</u> ask them for any references).

➢ Once you feel conversationally comfortable, the next level of "right people" will be individuals whom you know personally or who know other people who may be decision makers in their businesses (or are close to the decision maker level). In this case, you contact them and, again, simply tell them the truth…that <u>you are not looking for a job</u> and <u>have nothing to sell</u>. You would appreciate thirty minutes of their time to possibly surface some ideas that might grow their business and you would like their feedback on your approach. To eliminate any defensiveness, you can also assure them that if you do come up with any ideas they like, <u>they will be welcome to them</u>!

As in the first practice sessions, you should, prioritize them on how well you know them or that your referencing person knows them. You may begin to find some possibilities for work in the group, but practice and networking contacts are your primary objectives and you should again complete 3-4 actual interviews.

➤ When you have completed this group of 8-10 interviews, you should be ready to approach the additional networking contacts you have begun to identify through the networking activities in which you have been engaged during your practice sessions.

➤ To many of us, networking is not initially comfortable but the processes included <u>do work</u>. Just don't "overload your wagon" starting out and become discouraged. Start with the people you are most comfortable with, tell them the truth, and just "follow the yellow brick road to the wizard's castle."

It is truly simple, but most folks fall by the wayside just as it begins to produce results. Don't be one of them. Don't be just another reactive unemployed "casualty."

These tools here are <u>proven many times over</u>. Use them!

What is Networking?

Networking is an organized way to link contacts together to form a net of people who can give you support, advice and information. It means developing a broad list of contacts—people you've met through various social and business functions to gain exposure and possibly unearth promising opportunities.

<u>The best place to start developing your network is with your personal contacts</u>: family, friends, neighbors, business acquaintances, former classmates and professors, church associates, etc. Your goal in connecting with these people is to expand your network of contacts by asking everyone you know for a referral, while emphasizing that you <u>are not trying to sell anything</u>!

Networking can be done in a private, one-on-one meeting with an individual or in a group setting such as a business/association meeting. Whatever the method, the goals are the same:

Get your message out.

Gather beneficial information.

Leave a positive, lasting impression.

Get referrals to continue expanding your network.

Today, outplacement sources say that between 75 and 80 percent of new jobs are found through networking! As discussed, the traditional methods – a "solution looking for a problem" – are continuing to weaken and relationship-based contract/consulting project work will <u>absolutely</u> <u>require</u> proactive networking.

Current Average Statistics for New Job Acquisitions[*]

Rehire 4%

Recruiter 6%

Networking 78%

Internet Posting 5%

Newspaper Ad 2%

Staffing Agency 3%

Other 2%
(Direct Application, Job Fair, Newsletter, etc.)

[*]outplacement sources

Building a Network

Who from my family can help?

- Parents _____
- In-laws _____
- Sisters _____
- Brothers _____
- Others _____

Who from my old jobs can help?

- Former employees/employers _____
- Fellow workers _____
- Customers/clients _____
- Former competitors _____
- Others _____

Who from my school days can help?

- Sorority/fraternity friends _____
- Schoolmates _____
- Alumni associates _____
- Teachers, professors _____
- University officials _____
- Others _____

Who from my church can help?

- ➢ Fellow members_____
- ➢ Church leaders_____
- ➢ Sunday school teachers_____
- ➢ Ushers_____
- ➢ Officers_____
- ➢ Others_____

Who have I met via my hobbies that can help?

- ➢ Club members_____
- ➢ Card groups_____
- ➢ Sports (bowling, golf, tennis)_____
- ➢ Athletic clubs_____
- ➢ Others_____

Who do I know through my children?

- ➢ Teachers_____
- ➢ Parents of their playmates_____
- ➢ Coaches_____
- ➢ PTA_____
- ➢ Others_____

Who do I know through public service/charitable interests?

- ➤ Community Fund _____
- ➤ Chamber of Commerce _____
- ➤ Volunteer Associations _____
- ➤ YMCA/YWCA _____
- ➤ Others _____

What other professionals do I know?

- ➤ Doctors _____
- ➤ Dentist _____
- ➤ Accountant _____
- ➤ Lawyer _____
- ➤ Banker _____

Evaluate Your Networking Skills

Reflect on a recent professional or social event you attended. Answer the following thirteen questions honestly. Rate yourself on a score from 1–3.

1 = not at all   2 = to some extent   3 = did it

1. Did you come to the event dressed appropriately to present a positive image?

    1   2   3

2. Did you initiate a conversation with at least ten people?

    1   2   3

3. Did you introduce yourself using good eye contact, a sincere smile, a firm handshake, while providing a brief introduction of who you are?

    1   2   3

4. When conversing, did you listen closely for common interests and special needs?

    1   2   3

5. Were you open-minded to persons who may have looked, talked, or acted unlike those you tend to relate to?

    1   2   3

6. Did you actively listen for clues to each person's special strengths and abilities?

                1   2   3

7. Did you convey enthusiasm, energy and direction through your conversation?

                1   2   3

8. Did you let others know your expertise or special skills?

                1   2   3

9. Did you mingle throughout the room?

                1   2   3

10. Did you make a point of introducing any person you talked with to anyone else?

                1   2   3

11. Did you exchange business cards or telephone numbers?

                1   2   3

12. Have you followed up on each significant contact with a telephone call or personal note?

                1   2   3

13. If this was a business event, did you read recent periodicals to gather industry information prior to the meeting?

                1   2   3

Tips for Successful Business Networking

Effective business networking is the linking of individuals who, through trust and relationship building, become walking, talking advertisements for one another.

- <u>Keep in mind, networking is about being genuine and authentic</u>. The goal of networking is building trust and relationships, while seeing how you can help others.

- <u>Determine your goals for participating in networking meetings</u>. You should pick groups that will help you get the type of project or employment you desire. Some meetings are based more on learning, making contacts, and/or volunteering rather than on strictly making business connections.

- <u>Visit as many groups as possible that spark your interest</u>. What is the tone and attitude of the group? Do the people sound supportive of one another? Does the leadership appear competent? Many groups will allow you to visit two or three times before joining.

- <u>Ensure that the group is professional in its approach and conduct</u>. Ask these questions for yourself and to yourself: Does the group I am considering have a purpose, meeting agenda and time limit? (Do they stick to it?) Is there exclusivity (Is it negotiable?)? Is there "value"? Does any of this matter?

- <u>Hold</u> <u>volunteer</u> <u>positions</u> <u>in</u> <u>organizations</u>. This is a great way to stay visible and give back to groups that have helped you.

- <u>Ask</u> <u>open-ended</u> <u>questions</u> <u>in</u> <u>networking</u> <u>conversations</u>. This means questions that ask who, what, where, when, and how as opposed to those that can be answered with a simple yes or no. This form of questioning opens up the discussion and shows listeners that you are interested in them.

- <u>Become</u> <u>known</u> <u>as</u> <u>a</u> <u>powerful</u> <u>resource</u> <u>for</u> <u>others</u>. When you are known as a strong resource, people remember to turn to you for suggestions, ideas, names of other people, etc. This keeps you visible to them.

- <u>Have</u> <u>a</u> <u>clear</u> <u>understanding</u> <u>of</u> <u>what</u> <u>you</u> <u>do</u> <u>and</u> <u>why</u> <u>you</u> <u>do</u> <u>it</u>. It is essential that you can communicate clearly what makes you better, special and different from others doing the same thing. In order to get referrals, you must first have a clear understanding of what you do that you can easily articulate to others.

- <u>Be</u> <u>able</u> <u>to</u> <u>articulate</u> <u>what</u> <u>you</u> <u>are</u> <u>looking</u> <u>for</u> <u>and</u> <u>how</u> <u>others</u> <u>may</u> <u>help</u> <u>you</u>. Too often people in conversations ask, "How may I help you?" and no immediate answer comes to mind.

- <u>Follow through quickly and efficiently on referrals you are given</u>. When people give you referrals, your actions are a reflection on them. Respect and honor that and your referrals will grow.

- <u>Call those you meet who may benefit from what you do and vice versa</u>. Express that you enjoyed meeting them, and ask if you could get together and share ideas.

- <u>Hook up and form alliances with businesses that are complementary</u>. For example, if you are a real estate agent, network with attorneys and mortgage brokers. Remember, when networking always take your connection beyond the group level to the personal relationship level.

Close contact networking may well be the right technique at just the right time. In essence, it's a return to the old yet neglected concept of <u>relationship selling</u>. With the increasing clutter of direct mail and telemarketing as lead generating tools, and the sometimes offensiveness of cold calling, lead networking <u>can be the answer</u>, especially for individuals for whom <u>short term revenue is a must</u>!

Regardless of the situation, all of us have a choice…

To <u>Network</u> or <u>not work</u>!

9.
Finding the Need

"The one lesson I have learned is that there is no substitute for paying attention." — Diane Sawyer

I'd like to demonstrate how I generally present the Solutionship™ Process to a decision maker to whom I have been <u>referred</u>. (A <u>personal</u> contact is usually a little more protracted but virtually indentical.)

Once we get in front of them, there are several things that I must remember…

As said, in <u>every case,</u> the interaction <u>has to be simply a conversation</u>. The minute it slides towards a pitch, the door will begin closing: <u>nobody likes to be sold.</u> I reinforce this by repeating this statement – usually several times – something like, "I sincerely appreciate you taking your time to meet with me and I want to repeat that I am <u>not</u> here to sell you anything! I am not looking for a job or suggesting any type of magic bullet. I'd just appreciate a few minutes to talk to you about your business and see if we can find any opportunities in this crazy economy to grow your bottom line. So, please relax. I'd just like to ask a few questions about your business…Okay?"

If the answer is yes (and it usually is), I pull out my legal pad and begin.

This simple, proactive approach accomplishes several very positive things up front. It positions me as the facilitator, and it places the prospect in the more comfortable position of not having to come up with any questions.

As said, the format follows the SWOT Analysis.

S – Strength

W – Weakness

O – Opportunities

T – Threats

The first question (strength) is designed to do nothing but make the partner comfortable talking about their business.

In my case, it is usually something like, "I know times are tough today, but, if you don't mind, talk to me about a few things that seem to be going pretty well for you right now."

I want to <u>encourage</u> them <u>to</u> <u>brag</u> and to get us to a point where I can genuinely compliment them. I then transition to the (W) area, where we begin looking for <u>needs/opportunities.</u>

When we feel we are there, I say something like, "That's great! Congratulations. I can certainly understand why you're proud of that…but, while we're here, talk to me a little about a few areas where you might see some room for improvement." (Usually we will begin to see some things I <u>know</u> I can help with…and the temptation is to jump in and to <u>fix</u> <u>it</u>! But as we've said, it is <u>almost</u> **<u>always</u>** <u>the</u> <u>wrong</u> <u>thing</u> <u>to</u> <u>do</u>!)

Solutions are <u>always</u> best developed when the prospect is <u>jointly</u> <u>engaged</u> <u>and</u> <u>has</u> <u>a</u> <u>strong</u> <u>sense</u> <u>of</u> <u>ownership!</u> <u>It</u> <u>must</u> <u>be</u> <u>their</u> <u>idea!</u>

Several years ago, I was excited about getting an appointment with the CEO of a company that I knew was a perfect fit.

After rushing through a "very professional pitch covering my exceptional background and expertise," I charged right in and asked him to tell me about his problems, and he, surprisingly, started <u>telling</u> <u>me</u>. I snatched the conversation back from him and launched into an aggressive pitch of what, based on my experience, he should be doing. I'll never forget what happened.…

He raised his hand for me to stop, and looked at his watch. For a few seconds, things went deathly quiet. Then he said, "Ben, I've been in this business for twenty-seven years…you've been in my office for about fifteen minutes…I don't give a (blank) if you worked with the great Coca-Cola Company.® Do you think that us folks out here in the sticks can't come up with any good ideas on our own?

With that, he looked at his watch again, and said, "If you'll excuse me, I have another appointment." Then <u>he got up and he left me sitting in his office</u>!

But, <u>now I was in complete control</u>.

Needless to say, a project was not forthcoming.

Hopefully, you can learn from some of my mistakes and know when to shut up, when to take notes, and when to <u>let them be in charge.</u>

* * *

Back to finding the need…as soon as we begin to discuss opportunities, they may see some room for improvement. I start taking <u>detailed</u> notes… <u>verbatim!</u>

As I mentioned earlier, this is the "red meat" section of the conversation and my purpose is to get them to open up and discuss almost anything that comes to mind. But, I want to help them surface <u>only</u> two or three of their most pressing issues.

I do not want the menu to be so large that priorities become an issue. In my experience, I have found that the first couple are the most important.

Unless the need/opportunity is so pressing that the prospect is ready to sign on the spot, I <u>don't</u> <u>let</u> <u>it</u> <u>become</u> <u>a</u> <u>problem-solution</u> <u>discussion!</u>

Also, most employers think their businesses are different, and a <u>quick</u> <u>solution</u> smells much like just another "off-the-shelf" item. They will want to be certain that their Solutionship™ Process partner is giving their situation significant and concerted thought before allowing the discussion of any real ideas.

Once we have detailed our primary needs, we transition to the "O" portion.

I usually say something like, "I really appreciate your sharing these things and I'd like to give them some real thought. But, before I leave, please talk to me about some opportunities that you see in your business <u>now</u> but are just not able to take advantage of." (These are similar to, but different from, the "W" topics but will be easier to discuss.)

Once completed, it sets up the closing question in the "T" portion of the discussion, which for me is simply, "Why...?" "Why are you not able to take advantage of these opportunities?" (This is almost always related to time, people, money, etc.)

This is the point in the conversation that is usually most difficult for many of us.

As we have said <u>several</u> times, although the

prospect may be expecting a solution, if possible, we just <u>do</u> <u>not</u> <u>want</u> <u>to</u> <u>go</u> <u>there</u>!

I simply try to appear as contemplative as this old redneck is able…I take a moment or two, and say something like, "This has been a <u>great</u> conversation. Let me make a suggestion…give me a day or so to really think about what we've discussed and come back to you with a few ideas <u>in</u> <u>writing</u> to see if we are anywhere close to being on the same page. (Again, this will not be a sales pitch.) Even if we come up with something you might be interested in, if you feel you have the internal resources, funds are an issue, or you just don't want to work with me, <u>the</u> <u>ideas</u> <u>are</u> <u>yours</u>. I am, honestly, here to <u>just</u> <u>help</u> <u>you</u> <u>in</u> <u>any</u> <u>way</u> <u>possible</u>."

I then set a time for the next visit (or an e-mail if in-person is not possible). I stand up, thank them, and <u>leave</u>!

I have found that leaving without discussing <u>any</u> solution(s) places me at an extremely positive psychological advantage.

One client once told me, "Ben, you left me leaning!"

The reason is that I am going to give their business some concerted thought…and any ideas will <u>not</u> appear to be off-the-shelf.

This approach is professional, sensitized to business needs and helpful, with no attempt to control it, and it should result in <u>their</u> <u>ideas</u> <u>and</u> <u>their</u> <u>solutions</u>…<u>arrived</u> at <u>together</u>.

Okay, if we have found the needs, how do we fill them?

10.
Filling the Need

"Obstacles are those frightful things you see when you take your eyes off your goal." — H. Ford

I set my next appointment or my e-mail session within the next two to four working days if possible.

The minute I walk out the door, phones will begin to ring, e-mail will ding, fax will start grinding, the next appointment will come in…they will be back into the busy-ness of business…our discussions, no matter how exciting, will rapidly fade into the past. We <u>must</u> proactively stay top of mind!

And this next step is probably the simplest.

Writing a Proposal

Whatever your opinion of the problem may be, <u>you have to take into account your client's perceptions and accommodate them in your proposal</u>. Moreover, your proposal should be written as a set of suggestions addressing both the problem and its solution. These suggestions are based on your understanding of the information.

Unless you are responding to a formal proposal request, which specifies the format, your proposal should be typed on your stationery – either in the form of a letter or a memorandum – and could include the following:

- A title written as a one-sentence topic heading.

- A synopsis of the problem – supported by a brief analysis of documentation and including the client's own observations.

- A short statement of the suggested course of action.

- A brief statement of the benefits to the client by following the course of action you recommend.

- A description of the need for your recommended course of action, <u>using the client's own words as much as possible</u>!

- An outline of the first step(s) or action; a proposal which typically includes gathering further information.

- An estimate of the time and cost for the first stage of the project whenever possible.

This one page note should simply contain the basic elements for a continued conversation around the ideas you come up with together.

If the next session is face-to-face, I bring two copies of the note and I tell my client/partner that I have given the situation a good deal of thought and, as promised, have written down some ideas. Handing them their copy, I ask them if we could take a few minutes going over it together and seeing if we are anywhere close to being on the same page.

Once this is completed, I put the ball back in their court and <u>make</u> <u>them</u> <u>responsible</u> <u>for</u> <u>the</u> <u>close.</u>

If the session is email, I set a time for the conversation, ask them to print out a hard copy, and explain why…then I take them back through it on the phone.

Here is a sample format that I have used successfully in the past:

Dear Fred,

I sincerely appreciated our time together and, based on some of the things you told me, I am convinced that there are a couple of opportunities here that could definitely warrant more discussion.

As you told me,

- (in his/her words…a thumbnail of two or three ideas surface in conversation.)

- _____

- _____

Based on my experience, if consideration makes sense here is what it might look like:

Deliverables	Time Frames
(Discovery Outline)	(1 – 2) weeks?
(Plan Development…)	(2) weeks?
(Plan Implementation…)	(4) weeks?
Metrics	(ongoing)
*Investment Range	_____

(* If appropriate)

<u>Fred</u>, I am excited by these opportunities and truly look forward to working together if we get on the same page.

In any case, I do think they should be considered.

Respectfully,

Ben Hudson

Remember, during the conversation, you wrote down the opportunities verbatim. It has been my experience that the ideas then become their ideas and their ownership makes the whole process assume a very positive perspective. As simple as this seems, it is proven to be effective, and <u>strangely enough, very unusual</u>!

11.
Pricing

At some point in every conversation, pricing will probably surface, usually with a question by the client like, "How do you charge?"

The answer should always be, "It's probably premature to talk about now, because as I said, I am not here today to sell <u>a thing</u>. As you know, I have nothing to sell at this point. I always prefer to work on a project basis because it is a 'win-win' for everyone. You know exactly what you're getting and how long it will take, and I get a clear job description with a bit of time and flexibility."

Price Determination

When asking about price, the client is usually looking of an hourly or daily rate. Unless pressed extremely hard, <u>you</u> <u>do</u> <u>not</u> <u>want</u> <u>to</u> <u>give</u> <u>them</u> <u>one</u>. The reasons are simple and pragmatic. A project price is a "win-win". Nobody gets unnecessarily distracted by arrival time, quitting times, days worked, etc.

However, to determine a project price you will need to have an approximate hourly rate in mind.

The rule of thumb for arriving at a starting point is as follows:

1) Come up with an annual amount that you would consider fair if you consulted/contracted for an entire year.

2) Double that amount.

3) Divide the total by 2,000.

4) This will give you an hourly rate to start the process.

example: $100K x 2 = $200K ÷ 2,000 = $100/hour

Remember, the objective in this entire process is to get your foot in the door. In negotiation you can discount. (Let them know you are discounting.) But my recommendation is to very seldom do business pro bono. Everyone values "skin in the game."

12.
Closing the Deal

"When you get to a fork in the road, take it!"
— Yogi Berra

Years ago, when I started taking my first sales courses a lot of emphasis was placed on closing the sale. There were initial closes, trial closes, final closes and on and on....

In today's market, closing has become more of an art than a method, and certainly has to be more sensitive to the decision maker's needs than ever before.

The approach that I am recommending has been very successful, but honestly, I just backed into it myself.

Project consulting, my primary income source for over twenty years, is just a series of small jobs as opposed to one big job, and the job search process is almost identical...it's just done many more times. A few years back, I began to see my close rate decline as people became more experienced with traditional closing methods.

Following one particularly frustrating session, I became a bit short tempered and blurted out, "Well, if I haven't convinced you of the direction you ought to go, what do <u>you think next steps</u> should be?"…and <u>he started telling me.</u>

Most of us don't like to be closed…so I just decided to <u>stop</u>…and it worked!

So, when we have walked together through the notes and I feel that we are, in fact, close to being on the same page, I just bop the ball right back to them by making a comment like, "It appears to me that we might be fairly close to being on the same page, would you agree?"

If the answer is yes, or positive, I simply ask, "Well, what do you think the next steps are?" …and if they begin responding, I know I've at least gotten a bite, and I just follow the suggestions/thoughts from there.

If the answer is less positive, but still a bit open, my answer is, "What additional information would you need to help?"

I set a time frame and start putting it together.

If the answer is negative, I tell them that I certainly understand their reasons and I will write them a note outlining our discussion and the reasons for not moving forward.

I clearly <u>place the close in their hands,</u> and in each of the situations, <u>I lay the foundation to keep the door open.</u>

Over the years, many opportunities have resurfaced at truly unexpected times.

* * *

Just remember three words… <u>I never close.</u>

<u>They are the decision makers</u>, and I am there for <u>only one reason</u>…<u>to help them!</u>

13.
Summary

If you remember little else from this discussion, just keep this page in mind. I can personally guarantee you that it will pay dividends.

- Even after we come out the other side of these economic times, the employment process as we have known it will be forever changed.

- You <u>can</u> be extremely successful in today's job market, but all "solutions looking for a problem" no longer sell.

- You should present yourself as a partnership solutions provider with a helping mindset rather than a selling one.

- Your mantra should always be: <u>Find</u> the <u>Need</u> and <u>Fill It</u>. This will keep the process simple and allow your partner to clearly be the hero.

- <u>You must clearly demonstrate your value</u>…your R.O.I.

- You must understand that in most cases a contracting and/or project consulting relationship will be the <u>best way to both short term income and potential permanent employment.</u>

- Your presentation must be conversational, and

this only comes from practice. The best people to practice on are the folks who you know the best.

Finally, the Solutionship™ Process is <u>proven</u> <u>to</u> <u>work</u> and there is little need to re-invent the wheel. Learn it, practice it, and make it a habit! It will position you as exceptionally professional, truly caring, and a valuable employee!

14.
Making Habits

Aristotle said, "We are what we repeatedly do. Excellence, then, is not an act, but a habit."

Stephen Covey, author of *Seven Habits of Highly Effective People,* tells us that our character, basically, is a composite of our habits…and he defines a habit as the intersection of <u>knowledge, skill,</u> and <u>desire</u>.

Knowledge is the *what to do* and the *why.*

Skills are the *how to do….*

And desire is the *want to do….*

He tells us that we have to have all of them to make something a habit in our lives and that it requires work in all three areas…<u>but knowledge and skill have virtually no value without desire</u>. Desire is the ignition of the motor of habit building. Unless it is turned on and stays on, the engine never starts up, or it may simply sputter briefly and die.

This is possible because of the unique ability of humans for self-awareness (i.e., being able to think about the thought process itself), and it permits us to make choices about how we use our skills. We are not a prisoner of our feelings, our moods or our instincts. We can evaluate and learn from experience, both ours and others, and we can choose to make and break our habits. They are not predetermined by any of the accepted social maps:

1) Ancestral determinism (your grandparents did it)

2) Parental determinism (your parents did it)

3) Cultural determinism (someone/thing around you did it).

Although we are all somewhat affected by these factors, the bottom line is that we <u>can make choices and act on them</u> when they are appropriate. A successful life appears to be the result of simply choosing to do the "next right thing"…from moment to moment.

This leads us to Covey's first habit of highly effective people…<u>Be Positive</u>.

Productivity, however, results from more than merely taking the initiative. It means being responsible for our lives. We <u>must know</u>, with certainty, that <u>our behavior is a function of our decisions,</u> not our conditions. We can subordinate our feelings to our values. We must demonstrate both initiative and responsibility to make good things happen.

Covey also suggests that we look at the word responsibility (response-ability)…don't become victims of our circumstances, conditions or conditioning. Choose behavior based on values, rather than reacting in response to feelings.

Reactive people, either by conscious decision or by default, empower their conditions to drive them. Reactive people are victims of their particular social weather and build their emotional lives around the behavior of others…empowering the weaknesses of others to control them! They are not "response-able." They are hopeless, helpless victims who look at every change as personally threatening and every new day with frightening apprehension.

As we said, even proactive people <u>can</u> be influenced by external stimuli, but their response to this stimuli can be a "value leased" decision…and, as a rule, proactive people are the happy, energized, positive doers in our society…on top of life and comfortable wherever they might be…it is a choice!

Finally, Covey tells us that proactive people work on the things they <u>can</u> <u>do</u> <u>something</u> <u>about</u>, and the nature of their energy is positive…enlarging and magnifying…causing their circle of influence to grow continuously.

So…ask yourself…where are you on the reactive-proactive spectrum? In truth, we are all probably always moving somewhere along this spectrum… but Covey, our historical experience and plain common sense tells us that the habit of proactivity is the capstone…the foundational building block upon which all of Covey's other "six" habits rest!

Fortunately, we each have the Creator-given ability within us to <u>choose</u>…to become more proactive…to become more response-able…and to become more… PRODUCTIVE. There is no question regarding the effectiveness of the Solutionship™ Process and, if "the dumbest guy in the room" can do it, you can do it too. So, just <u>choose</u> <u>to</u> <u>do</u> <u>it</u> <u>yourself</u>. You will be amazed at the gifts you have been given!

The traditional résumé driven job search method is <u>reactive!</u> The Solutionship™ Process of "Finding the Needs and Filling Them" is cutting edge proactive.

There is <u>no</u> <u>shortage</u> of needs today.

You are holding the tools proven to help <u>fill</u> <u>them</u>!

<u>CHOOSE</u> <u>PROACTIVITY</u>…<u>CHOOSE</u> <u>SUCCESS</u>…<u>AND</u> <u>MAKE</u> <u>IT</u> <u>A</u> <u>HABIT.</u>

Believe me, again, if I can do it, you can do it.

The Author
Ben Hudson

Ben started in the Consumer Products industry over thirty years ago. He began his career in corporate development and international advertising. His passion is business and entrepreneurial development.

Ben established Business Development Associates, a management consulting firm focused on new business start-ups and renewal, growth and development for established corporations. In addition, he developed the Entrepreneurial Program at Lee Hecht Harrison (Atlanta) and implemented that program for over twelve years. This entrepreneurial program, a unique blend of proven practical experience in Sales/Sales Management, Marketing, Advertising, Promotions, Public Relations and Organizational Development has been a success model for the Lee Hecht Harrison organization and recognized as one of the most comprehensive in the outplacement industry.

Ben has a treasure trove of experience: He has assisted more than 1,500 individuals considering self employment and has been instrumental in over 250 small business start-ups becoming profitable entities.

Ben was a founder of the first successful sales promotion group within an international advertising agency. As a group product manager with the Coca Cola Company® he had full responsibility for four major international brands, growing brand Sprite to the leadership position within the overall lemon-lime category. In a consulting capacity, he has successfully assisted with the growth/repositioning/sale/merger of a number of national organizations.

Ben is a graduate of the University of Georgia and has completed MBA studies programs at Harvard Business School. He is a former Board Member of the Atlanta Institute of Management Consultants. Currently he is coaching, training, and consulting clients.

RESOURCES

Books & Magazines

201 Ways Great Ideas for Your Small Business, Jane Applegate

Selling the Invisible: A Field Guide to Modern Marketing, Harry Beckwith

The Complete Guide to Consulting Success, Howard Shenson, Ted Nicholas

The E-Myth Revisited, Michael Gerber

The Millionaire Next Door, Thomas J. Stanley, Ph.D., William D. Danko, Ph.D.

Rich Dad, Poor Dad, Robert T. Kiyosaki

The Origins of Entrepreneurship, Jeff Timmons

Guerilla Marketing, Jay Conrad Levinson

Good to Great, Jim Collins

101 Ways to Promote Yourself, Raleigh Pinskey

Free Agent Nation, Daniel H. Pink

The Well Fed Writer, Peter Bowerman

Fast Company Fast Company (magazine)

Websites, Tools & Newsletters

www.tompeters.com

www.actionplan.com – marketing assessment tools

www.freeconference.com – free conference call bridge lines

www.paypal.com – cost-effective tool for accepting credit card payments

www.mollyguard.com – free tool to manage workshop registrations, collect fees

www.surveymonkey.com – free survey templates to poll clients, experts

www.pollmonkey.com – use on your website for quick polls and to make it interactive

www.ideamarketers.com – content source for ezines, newsletters, articles

www.livemeeting.com – conferencing free business web seminars

www.officedepot.com/webcafe - seminars - topics of interest to small businesses

www.wikipedia.org – the free encyclopedia that anyone can edit

www.mindjet.com – mind mapping tools

www.assistu.com – organization to find virtual assessments

www.smallbusinessportal.com – provides links to Internet sites helpful to small business researchers, policy makers and support agencies

E-Newsletters

www.constantcontact.com – create, manage, and distribute your own newsletters and announcements

www.ezinequeen.com – seminars, resources, marketing tips for small businesses

www.actionplan.com – marketing ideas for independent consultants

www.trendsight.com – gender-focused marketing strategies, marketing to women

Organizations & Associations

SCORE – Service Core of Retired Executives; www.score.org

Small Business Development Centers (usually affiliated with state universities)

Small Business Administration – www.sba.gov

American Marketing Association – www.ama.org

Women's Business Enterprise National Council (WBENC) – www.wbenc.org

Business Marketing Association – www.marketing.org

Publishers Marketing Association – www.pma-online.org

How Much Is Your Time Worth?

The following table calculates the actual hourly cost of time for people at various income levels. The value of each of your hours – even each of your *minutes*…is something to bear in mind when you review your diary record. Look at your time as money to invest. At your day-end summary, congratulate yourself for good investments…and also pinpoint any that may not bear as high a yield.

You are also investing the time of persons who report to you and other people whose time you consume. Consider those costs, too.

Salary Year	Salary Week	Benefits= 40% Total Salary	Total Week	Value Per Hour	Value Per Minute
$5,000	$96	$38	$135	$3	$0.06
6,000	115	46	162	4	0.07
7,000	135	54	188	5	0.08
8,000	154	62	215	5	0.09
9,000	173	69	242	6	0.10
10,000	192	77	269	7	0.11
15,000	288	115	404	10	0.17
20,000	385	154	538	13	0.22
25,000	481	192	673	17	0.28
30,000	577	231	808	20	0.34
35,000	673	269	942	24	0.39
40,000	769	308	1,077	27	0.45
45,000	865	346	1,212	30	0.50
50,000	962	385	1,346	34	0.56
55,000	1,058	423	1,481	37	0.62
60,000	1,154	462	1,615	40	0.67
65,000	1,250	500	1,750	44	0.73
70,000	1,346	538	1,885	47	0.79
75,000	1,442	577	2,019	50	0.84
80,000	1,538	615	2,154	54	0.90
85,000	1,635	654	2,288	57	0.95
90,000	1,731	692	2,423	61	1.01
95,000	1,827	731	2,558	64	1.07
100,000	1,923	769	2,692	67	1.12
125,000	2,404	962	3,365	84	1.40
150,000	2,885	1,154	4,038	101	1.68
175,000	3,365	1,346	4,712	118	1.96
200,000	3,846	1,538	5,385	135	2.24

Notes